Perplexed Skin

Patrick Cotter

Perplexed Skin

ARLEN HOUSE

Published in 2008 by
ARLEN HOUSE
an imprint of Arlen Publications Ltd
PO Box 222
Galway
Phone/Fax: 353 86 8207617
Email: arlenhouse@gmail.com

Distributed in North America by
SYRACUSE UNIVERSITY PRESS
621 Skytop Road, Suite 110
Syracuse, NY 13244–5290
Phone: 315–443–5534/Fax: 315–443–5545
Email: supress@syr.edu

ISBN 978–1–903631–54–6, hardback, 2008
ISBN 978–1–903631–84–3, paperback, 2009
(a signed and numbered limited edition is also available)

House Editor ¦ Susan Bennett
Typesetting ¦ Arlen House
Printing ¦ Betaprint
Cover Image ¦ Patrick Cotter

the arts council
an chomhairle ealaíon

Contents

ACKNOWLEDGEMENTS

Grateful acknowledgement is made to the editors of the following periodicals where these poems have appeared:

An Múinteóir: 'Forebearance'
Ars Interpres: 'Bookworm'
College Green: 'In Summer's Heat'
The Cork Review: 'An Insensitive History of Japan', 'Laurence Corcoran 1910–1995', 'Nightfeed'
The Cork Literary Review: 'Advances', 'Measured'
Cuaderno del Madrid: 'The Revenge of the Lilies'
The Echo Room: 'A Rhineland Suite'
The Erotic Review: 'A Contemporary Catullus on Cunnilingus'
The Irish Times: 'Arco'
Oxford Magazine: 'Margaret Corcoran neé Kirwin'
Oxford Poetry: 'Party for Innocents, May 1971'
Poetry Durham: 'Forebear'
Poetry Ireland Review: 'Californian Girl', 'April 1999', 'On Garryvoe Beach', 'The Lure of Night', 'Purchased Wisdom'
The Salmon: 'Confessions of a Nightporter'
The SHOp: 'The Poet Contemplates Book Cover Portraits', 'The Monument', 'Song of Songs', 'Wereteen'
Southword: 'Soul After Death', 'A Tigress is ...'

And to the following anthologies:
David Marcus (ed.) *The Irish Eros* (Dublin, Gill and Macmillan, 1996)
Maddalena Vacana (ed.) *Poeti D'Europa* (Alvito, Italy, Centro Studi Letterari, 2005)
Irene De Angelis & Joseph Woods (eds.) *Our Shared Japan* (Dublin, Dedalus Press, 2007)

The author is grateful to the Arts Council for Travel Awards in 2003, 2006 and 2007.

for Oisín and Romy

Perplexed Skin

A Bodega Suite

1: Preise dem Engel die Welt

A bonsai-sized angel lies
asleep in my shopping bag,
wings curled in on itself,
either a handsome she or a pretty young he.
It snores harp strings in no particular tune
but in a pleasant calming hum
which attracts the dusky, snub-nosed brunette
from across the vastness of table sixteen.
She looks from me to the bag and back,
perplexed, slightly anxious.
Her mouth opens to speak, but shuts
soundlessly. She knows me not
and returns to her broadsheet's miniscule print
with lessened concentration, nostrils flexing.
I wonder what noise the angel makes
when it awakes: it's been asleep since I bought it
along with the box of angel food.

2: Homage to Duchamp

Not having drunk enough of anything today,
I stand by the urinal, piss dark and dense trickling from me.
Gone are the golden showers of youth when a stream
would arc high into the air with all the force of a water canon.
Gone are the days of schoolboy pissing contests;
Beside me stands a ghost envious of any piss at all.
The ghost is a new ghost: this bar is only ten years old.
But already he's old enough for me to sniff
at his outmoded fashion sense, his serpentinely thin leather tie,
his ballooning baggy trousers, everything permeable as mist.
I step through him on my way to the hand-basin,
hoping I'll have somewhere nicer to haunt,
something more congenial to be envious of
when I stop pissing forever.

3: Sometimes a Freud is Just a Freud

There is a beech-wood diver over my head
fissuring from ass to crown.
Chains attached to each foot hold her
to the ceiling but cannot hold her together.
This is the second time she has started to fall apart.
Some years ago she split in two,
each side twirled around, turning its back on the other.
The left side had no idea what the right side was up to.
I could sit somewhere else but I like,
from my angle of view, the placement
of the triangle of her nose in the valley of her breasts,
and I know it won't last much longer.
Her outstretched hands are facing hockey sticks;
geometry and symmetry fisticuffing
the sculptor's mistaken intentions.

4: A Richard Brautigan Moment

'Are you writing a new poem?' said the Japanese girl
her hair shimmering like a dark undiscovered continent.

I'm trying, musing over odd vacant imaginings,
distracted by the jungle beat of the bar's soundtrack
which shakes the potted palm leaves by my side.
'I'm trying', I say, above the underfed baby's wails.
Sometimes the words come more easily here
than in a silent room. The indiscernible voices,
multiple exhalations, clattering of glass and cups,
if not inspirational, are at least companionable,
making the great trek through the word-veldt
less lonesome. Maybe I should have said all this
rather than just 'I'm trying'.

What I said turned her round like a self-correcting,
Sony robotic puppy hitting the skirting board.

5: Free WiFi

Every little corner of her face,
framed by the edges of our laptops is perfect.
Having studied her full face too long
without being able to talk to her
my heart is sore
so I take portions of her face
rearranging the margins of the laptops
like a setsquare.
Her unplucked brows
are like *sosho* strokes
over narrow hooded eyes.
Her mouth, the crevice between
two wine-stained cherry petals.
Her nose's ridge
higher than average for her race
straight as a sword.
Her jawline sharp enough
to cut the souls of men
who cannot hold her.

6: Mistaken for August Strindberg

The Swede who brings my drinks
is as personable as she is pretty
until I ask her out.
'Where would you take me?'
she snaps suspiciously.
'Not far', says I, 'We could
go as far as the upstairs bar'.
'The Green Rooms?'
'Yes, or the White Rooms',
says I, hoping variety of choice
would lead to assent.
'You know there are two hundred
and thirty seven other bars in this town?'
'Yes', says I, astonished at her encyclopedic knowledge,
'but all without you, an angel, a ghost
and a schisming beech-wood diver'.
She looks at me as if I had two heads
or at least as if the one head I had
was made of reconstituted wood-shavings.
'You know, I used to think you were nice',
she said, before turning on her heel
with the grace of a reindeer.

Ovid's Elegy No. 5

1: In Summer's Heat ...

After lunch in August swelter,
prone upon a narrow cot;
sunrays fingering through a welter
of blinds, Venetian, metal, hot:
a simulacrum of forest dapple light,
or the shade of day kissing night.

In such shade might a blushing, reticent,
schoolgirl debut in a discotheque.
In strode Corinna, dripping, magnificent,
dreadlocks stroking her glistening neck;
as proud and brazen as Kate Moss
striding a catwalk, radiating gloss.

Her showering-gown hung airily agape.
Stirred-up enough, I rawly seized
its cuffs, grabbing like a baited ape.
Feigning modesty she smiled and teased,
then momentarily faked a headache,
then dropped her gown as in mistake.

Her naked sight made my torpid brain swirl.
Not one blemish on her skin, not a zit
could I see as she turned in a twirl.
Whoa! My fingers on her pert, neat, tit.
My cheek on her shoulder of little fat,
her geodesic buttock and her stomach flat.

No need to list you more ... she was swell.
In fervid humour she pulled, down we fell.
You easily can guess the rest. Well,
if such moments happen only once, eternity's hell.

2: Corinna's Take

How such an indolent bastard
acquired such Nureyev-shaped pins
I'll never know, but as they laid
knees down in the musty cot

light slicing his body like best Sheffield
I wanted to run my tongue
over his contoured, downy outline,
see him turn slowly like Johnny Depp

in my daydreams and unfold his
broad shoulders like wings,
feel hands used to spinning
rhymes, spin my brain

with their snake-like enwrapments.
But he woke too soon and almost
froze me with the gormlessness
of his Pavlovian eagerness.

The gown I had started to drop
I retied with a breathless growl.
I was cut-up by his bluntness.
That's when he grabbed me

and I giggled at his idiocy.
He had me then and it was only ok.
He fell asnoring afterwards, plonker.
Thank God it's not like this every time.

An Insensitive History of Japan

The history of Japan is as complex
as the history of Western sculpture,
one period is Henry Moore to another's Michaelangelo
and occasionally Giacometti comes sharply
into play like ritual disembowelment.
These thoughts clutter my unZenned mind
sitting at the Triskel Arts Centre's new sushi bar.

Later, raw fish on my tongue makes me think
of all the Japanese women I will never know;
all one hundred million of them;
from the EFL students in their slinky black clothes
to the war widows in their grieving kimonos.

NO LASSO

Preparatory Drawing

You are more than a nervous mare,
shaping flutes of beautiful steam
through your nostrils in a chilled field.
But sometimes coming near you
I feel like your friend who approached
the handsome stallion without poise or care
and instead of winning him over
merely scared him with the simplest
little movements of his harmless hands.

Oil on Canvas

Shaping flutes of beautiful steam
through your nostrils in a cold stream
you are more than a reticent, nervous mare,
but sometimes, awkwardly coming near,
I feel like your friend who, devoid of care
or poise, approached the handsome stallion
and instead of impressing the hooved rapscallion,
merely frightened him with the simplest motions
of his harmless hands, with his unsure emotions.

Song of Songs

> And I don't think it far-fetched to draw a comparison
> between the making of love and the making of Eucharist.
> – Rev. Jim Cotter, *Pleasure Pain & Passion*

That night, reawakened, my spirit in flight, I sung
amid a frenzied supplication of palms and kisses;
the miracle of your lips on my neck, my tongue
in your ear: swords slashing-clear choked egresses.

My fingers overboard, walking the waves of your sides
each shudder a kinetic prayer of gratitude to a god
who saw me loveless for years. Your pelvic grides
almost unsheathing my rod of its Gossamer ephod.

Your eyes as blue and deep as the sea of Galilee,
the communion wafer whiteness of your skin,
evoke in me forever the fervour of a devotee.
Scent of your crannies, a sweet and spicy jasmine,

the secret, tactile offerings of your moles
in my mouth, metaphorical vocables of God's shout
pronouncing the sacredness of our eternal souls.
Sounds from your mouth were a holy oil poured out,

your vulva a tabernacle door, route of your devout
coming, God's coming, dispelling doubt.

In Good Taste

How we swived like wild roans
rushing with a river's wrath.
Afterwards we rested whacked-out bones;
our limbs a fleshy, drowsy wreath.

I lay awake all night to hear you breathe;
your heart the light metronome of a waif.
Enervation made my brain sap seethe
till sleep stole me off like a jealous wife.

As my mind slipped through the dreaming seal
my tongue still savoured labial cream.
Was this my first dream coming real
or our first real coming in a dream?

A Contemporary Catullus on Cunnilingus

I think of all the rubber-tipped pencils
I mouthed gently as a boy
not knowing how long and hard
my tongue practiced for this joy.

Hyperion Tragedy

I fell asleep and so, in dream, rose
As the envious sun, stealthily,
In little gleamings, which crept
The streets along, then penetrated

Your windows in shafts so bold
Your bedroom walls blazed white,
All shadows gone. Alone you lay
In tranquil dreams, I had no wish

To waken you, but sticky crusts
Of sleeping-sand melted
At my rays' soft brush. Your heart
Vibrated with a quickening rap,

Propelling your blood's sweet flow.
Your eyelids shuttered open,
Stirring the air with a feverish thresh;
Allowing me, in particles,

To dart along nerves to your soul
Where I lit up once more
Your reticent, retinal world.
You stretched your limbs

With the delicacy of a foal.
With a divine precision, borrowed
From beyond myself (a child
Of the unredemptive faithful),

I was your guide. Shambling
Sleepily from room to room
In your ordinarily shadowy home,
You mumbled, chiding yourself

In what you thought was private,
An hour of sacred solitude.
And then in a brilliance
More blinding than the sun

You shed your nightshirt
And the brightness of your body
Stood immense in all its
Unposed, unaffected state,

Grown yet more beautiful.
My fire – I dowsed with shame,
Distressed I made such solitude
An undeserving victim

Of prying, intrusive gawkings.
Your name, my forgetting of which
Is your desire, chrism on my lips,
Angina of my heart, my last word

As I shrouded my eyes in heavy-
Skirted nimbuses, rain falling
In torrents, raising a street-sward
Of daffodils and crocuses:

Crushings for cars and buses.

On Garryvoe Beach

Waves we sought spontaneously at sunrise
smashing us with their enveloping freeze,
froth sizzling about your neck like a spermy collar;
salt electrons subsiding to your covered breast;

more of the sea's power advancing in coils
flexing to be sprung on our tender cores;
the sea's jigging force fanatically spurring us
to dance, to gyrate with involuntary shivers.

We landed on our beach-head
of re-acquainting, our sinews in spasms.
In the purring car, under flimsy covers
our limbs chastely meshed for heat.

We pressed lightly against each other
like clueless innocents: making light
of our first embrace after years
of bitter estrangement.

Yet I knew this diffident new dance
would be threatened by kisses, exhilarating
and erosive as the sea, swelling inside me:
your warm white neck presented;
your lips, evermore, to one side.

Karl Liebknecht and Rosa Luxemburg and the Landwehr Canal Berlin 1919

for Frank O'Callaghan

Six months before the parade of boat and meathooks took
place
The water turned the colour of her name.
His body was a colander through whose holes
The blood gushed out while his guts were barely retained.
Her limbs stiffened to stone so the water ceased
murmuring
And became as still again as a mirror never looked in.

April 1999

When power corrupts, poetry cleanses.
– John F. Kennedy, *November 1962*

Days spirited past like a monitor's flicker.
All the while a heavy cable, slotted
into the serial port jutting from my neck,
had gone undetected by my left-hand cerebrum.

But the right side of my brain, eager to
display its smart-aleck capacity for plug-and-play,
related at breakfast how this connection alone
powered all NATO bombing in Serbia.

On television I saw a man use his severed leg
as a crutch and a boy feed his pet dog
his own shock-blasted German Shepherd eyes:
substitutes for embargoed *Pedigree Chum.*

In a fit of judicious revulsion
I ripped the cable away.
Immediately Americans started to fall
from the skies like fucked-out ant drones.

Sky News beamed pictures of
mid-West mammies moaning.
Shreds of yellow ribbons flickered
from blue-rinse locks like plaintive snow.

Before anyone could notice
and choose to erase my children
I tried to reconnect the wires
as if they were as simple

as the TV aerial bombarding me
with simplistic coverage all week;
but the filaments were too complex
the connectors too multitudinous.

After my efforts,
B52s flew upside down
Pershing missiles cruised backwards
like show-off sparrowhawks on e.

Californian Girl

for Beverly

You are the why of appetite.
More-of-you is beyond beautiful.
Love drips here and I drink.
Your mouth, the purse of my tongue,
your limbs lie quiet and musky on my drying skin.
No thoughts do I give now to your relentless warriors.
When alone, I hear their footfalls stamping towards infamy:
a hard chorus of hob-nailed leather
rapping over the planet's byways.
Earlier I swam through my own sweat to breach you,
to source your core, stripping away,
ripple by ripple, the lappings of pleasure.

If we should have a child, would he
roll in fear at the sound of your brothers' flight?
Whatever answer, I will love you,
even as the bayonet carves at my throat,
even as our son swathes himself in stars
and the colours of the barbershop,
sings allegiance to the dollar,
to the constitution of the bullet and the gun.

Blood in the Water

for Ly Seppel

At Käsmu these days
the only blood in the water
is the reflected red of the fading sun,
rouged-up like a pantomime dame
who knows she is on show.
At the same time, high in the trees,
over the retreat of the writers' union,
a snowy owl feeds her two adolescent chicks
almost as big as herself,
but still wailing like babies.
They sit as high as Soviet border guards
in the bad old days, plump
in their observation posts, groggy
from stomachs already filled,
while the little black mice
scurry through the undergrowth, desperate
to reach the asylum of a fallen pine
whose spindly branches are like outreaching arms
ready to save.

SURPLUS

Impossible, I think now, I could ever
have foreseen or even hoped for you.
I remember how once your breath rushed
the down of my neck like a wave.

I was breathless, but inviolate.
Blemishes on my skin, hot as spots of the sun:
love flared out wherever you gazed,
wherever you touched, spools of it,

love in surplus, love released.
Our moment of first meeting,
you standing in my doorway,
your blouse an unremembered shade,

your hat and coat charcoal grey,
but your eyes danced. No
amount of local drizzly weather
could detract from the glow of you.

Our moments passed into history
even as we lived them, etching themselves
into record somewhere between synapse and neuron,
leaving us, after all is done, a bequest of pulses,

chemical and wet, firing on eternal, wistful,
again.

Butterfly Girl

> You shouldn't have a mirror facing the bed directly,
> because mirrors that reflect the bed usually cause
> marriages to become rather complicated due to the
> presence – or entry – of a third party into the relationship
> – Lillian Too

A ritual that always thrilled me: your silly
dance, you nude in heels, shaking your toosh,
exiting the room for a final pee,
me smiling. Later with playful
preying movements you swooped over me,
nibbling my neck, nipples hard,
hot as little flames scorching my chest.
The mirror we did not place on the ceiling
moped in a corner, sheathed in dust.
Your mouth was a moist gourmet dessert,
your cave in flood before I got there.
Your skin: peach flesh undulating, shuddering
with firmness. You were too Asian to be smelly;
pungent aromas were my markings smeared on you;
while my groin, lips, flanks overloaded
with incredulous touch, the simple feel of you.
Meanwhile the mirror plotted, Feng Shui-wise
to lure you away into another dimension,
distant, far beyond earshot, impenetrable.

Jimmy Choo

Long, long ago
in my solitary kid-hood
I so loved my new Batman suit
I wore it to bed,
cape, utility belt, mask
with glow-in-the-dark eyebrows,
I can't remember what I felt:
pleasure in the perceived power of it
or glee at its sleekness.
All I remember is my father
turning into the green-haired Joker
screaming at me to take it off,
fearful I'd turn in my sleep and choke.
Weeks later I did it again.
He threw mask and cape in the fire,
plastic shapes curled-up in the flames
like fists before combustion.
Ashes scattered like vampires up the flue.

Tonight I've relented and let you take
your new stilettos to bed, watch you
stroke and sniff the vinegary leather,
watch the red patent of them
glow in your pupils as they interact
heliographically with your Revlon
nail polish, before you slip them
delicately over your feet like a muzzle
over a loved Labrador.
It takes ages for me to fall asleep,
all night long I sense their viciousness,
hear the sheet emit
a short whine as it's slit.
Morning I wake
and blearily believe
blood's on my chest,
until I feel the point
of your heel pressing on my Adam's apple,
you at the other end of the bed

raised on your elbows,
smile coming into focus.

Long Distance Lover

Not yet gaunt with age,
no longer peachy youthful,
at the airport my profile presses mild alarms:
I'm scruffily attired, a solitary traveller.
My bags are sifted through
as if scissors or tweezers were gold.
I stand calm as a Buddha,
my chest packed with incendiaries of feeling
no instrument detects.
One security guard, intuitively gifted,
flirts.

Seventeen

The sinuousness of his thoughts weaves a thread
through the space in front of him, through the rooms,
past the table-corners, over the windowsills
he and she brushed against, separately, together.
No seedy shop-bought aids assisted their lovemaking,
just the common surfaces of a common household
which he worships now for their ordinariness.
Light has travelled seventeen minutes further
since his cellphone face went dark.
He tastes her words still which fell
from loganberry lips he will never see
nor moisten again. He wonders and wonders hard
without wanting to bring his wondering to an end,
how did her words get here? Carried by beam
off satellite, through clouds, past asteroids
or slithered along the planet surface,
over fault lines, deep sea valleys, continental shelves?
The orchid he bought her, too delicate, too cumbersome
for transatlantic carriage, after two years
blooms in a constellation of yellow and lilac,
seventeen blossoms from one little pot.
Janis Ian lies silent in the CD rack in the corner.
His own ridiculously-innocent, adolescent face
smiles at him from an old photograph.

Bays luxuriated around us, broadcasting their pungency. It was years before I would read five of their leaves pinned to my pillow while chanting in sevens and counting in sevens a spell would conjure up my steadfast Valentine.

Too late now. We were absorbed by the corpses of the redwoods, as we strolled around looking first at this one, then at that, all of them felled in one direction away from the distant, self-annihilating mountain which had disappeared with nuclear force aeons before R.L. Stevenson first stood here and marvelled at it all; how the trees were made of stone, how the annihilating volcano had sculpted them, if not into its own image, indubitably of its own substance: the silica which had invaded every redwood cell reshaping its glittering self into each fold of exterior bark, all of a tree's concentric innards, recording forevermore in cutaway cross-sections the trees' happy and cruel years.

I was split in two like many of the trunks, marvelling on the one hand at their petrified plight, on the other hand at the company of your own luminous self. As an act of resolution I reached for the living, a sprig of California Bay, redolent; rolled it to brittle fragments in my palm, held it to your face to share, to see you smile at its scouring aroma.

If my soul could be sliced and petrified a huge ring of growth would show for this short-lived moment.

Sans Merci

My home dogless, but in my stomach
a ventriloquist who growls,
sometimes muttering cute little snarls
which still I associate with the crisp
bodhrán of your belly from where
I first heard them echo,
disbelieving your denials.
The light depression left by your ass
in my mattress has long since lifted,
but still the voice throws whimpers
from odd corners under the duvet,
anywhere than from his master's stomach.
Fido, I call him, my merciless little *Bauchgeist.*

Lassius Niger at Home

During December's shortened days,
ants scarper along my cracked countertop,
like flecks of animated demerera

or broken type poltergeisted,
each a scurrying link in the chain of themselves.
They prospect for crystals of processed beet

or mine the gold of spilt honey.
I am the unappreciated stoker
of radiated, indoor, winter heat.

Outdoors, ants huddle winterlong
in balls of tepid stupor.
My guests gesticulate with more limbs

than I have words to muster.
Somewhere sits a brooding queen,
a little Stalinness, paranoiac and protected,

the pulsing centre of her own cult,
spurting out newborn faster than I could kill.
Chaste from now till death:

one droning was enough for her.
With every daughter a royal taster
she is impossible to poison

in her unreachable bunker.
Once they laid siege to my aspidistra
with their captive aphids transforming

the plant's sap to a sweetened slurry
ants hoover-up. If they were bees,
come autumn they would sweep me

outdoors with their nest's detritus: desiccated
egg husks; the frameworks of discarded wings;
their own defenceless, offenceless, redundant brothers.

Winter cold would be their unappealable
barring-order. Someday my tolerance
will be as exhausted as my sugar-bowl.

THE SINGING BICHON

My dog sings arias but only to me.
Mahler's *Kindertotenlieder* he knows
imperfectly. The *In Paradisum*
of Fauré's requiem he renders
with a strong nasal strain.
He can't quite reach all the notes
of Purcell's *The Plaint*,
but hey, he's just a dog.

He began to sing
when I began to ignore him.
Neither of us can stand the other's company.
When he shakes his Bichon curls,
doggy whiffs tinged with bitter fermentations
assault the upper reaches of my nostrils.
His piss perfumes the corners of my living room
with a pungency made worse by the addition
(without obliteration) of the mop-bucket's
ammonia-based floor fluid.
I can't stand him because he smells.
He can't stand me because I'm impervious
to his plaintive, glistening eyes.

Regularly we each need to elude
the secret inner lives of our separate solitudes.
I, by listening to my music,
he by stepping outdoors to sniff
the arses of other dogs
or to beg attention of passing children.
After I ignored his whines to be let outside
he learnt to sing. That first night
I could not avoid paying attention
to his original interpretation
of Raphael Courteville's *Creep, creep, softly creep*
I released him. He arse-sniffed.

The following night I ignored his Courteville
and he sang something by Dureflé.
I once tried to arrange a soirée
where I planned to accompany him on cello,
my living-room too bijoux for the pianoforte,
but with the house full of guests
he had no solitude to escape
and no need to sing.
He doesn't know I know
he sings Rufus Wainwright
when he thinks I'm not around.
Smelly bastard.

A Rhineland Suite

for Daniel Schwarz

1: The Moral Objector

At night, revolving, the glowing Mercedes symbol
hovers above the city like a capitalist angel.

The Anarchist punk senses no admonishment,
since he is gothic with a face as grey as a pavement,

He doles out stickers which advise one to boycott
the impending census. I try to recall but forget

the moment I first saw youths, older than I, dressed
like this. They thought they had everything sussed.

I never knew mankiness could take such effort.
I needed neither time nor labour to look like dirt.

I imagine his disciplined father confused,
wondering where he went wrong or else amused,

declaring jokingly his son was a victim of war;
a gargoyle unperched from his high-up lair

during an air-raid on the cathedral of Köln.
His granite stone frame treads densely alone

till the next assault, the next *Putsch*
on the pinnacles of fashion when such

elements as feathers and red might reign
surreal in place of leather and black. Then

perhaps, a gothic cemetery might hire him out
as a mobile adornment for a poor person's vault,
or as a memorial for some Fritz Lang starlet.

2: On the Tram

With jingles and rasps we swerve along this street,
this tram and I, in this compact citadel of style:
Porsches, jewellers' shopfronts, more Porsches compete
with art arcades, silver-hued Mercs and gracile
girls for my eyes' regard. The tram slowly halts.
One graceful girl climbs on, dressed head to toe
in fashionable black, her eyes're impenetrable smalts,
her hair's in creeping tendrils, a luxuriant hedgerow,
a caresser of the dancing whorl of her ear, a blond
frame for her *Übermensch* face, mark of her race.
How is she not astounded by her own beauty? Franz, the fond
beetle, old scribbler, would have mused in my place.
I imagine his sisters, herded by men following duty,
with *Arbeit Macht Frei* in their eyes, their thoughts
miles from the nearest tramride and that girl's beauty,
their souls ascending into heaven in black smoky noughts.

3: Portrait of Young American Girl Düsseldorf 1987

Remember sitting comfy on the ground,
of the crowded, cobbled *Altstadt* street,
the roasting fowl on Heine's spits found
favour with our noses which moved our feet
to hasten us to ask for one whole sapid bird.
That chicken's tang still lingers on my tongue
as I recall a later time, same place, a third
chick settled herself down and wrung
her arms around me like a flourish-weed
swirling the bole of a clapped-out oak.
A drunken mouse (albino) full of greed
sipped quietly between her teeth, not coke,
but malt whiskey, vintage, seeped in peat.
The cooling breeze erected a neglected teat.

That afternoon Nazi youths with shaven heads,
fingers behind ears to resemble fools' crowns,
didn't quite goosestep or hop or cluck but spread
their limbs awkwardly in some drunken strut. Frowns
had no effect on their comportment. No Turks or Greeks
about they jeered at us who shared whiskey with a mouse.
We were 'arseholefucking, jewcocksucking, non-Aryan freaks'.
Her naked bellybutton became more rhythmic to arouse
those fascist pricks, to advertise what they couldn't touch,
nor could I. She gave me more to drink
but not from the same cup the rodent drank; no such
high-schoolish luck: she was about sixteen I think.
Her hair was corn-coloured, her irises green.
My drunken attraction for her, was, I know, obscene.

In a mirror her eyes have known no wrinkles;
only in a lover's face, her favourite crinkly;
her name for aging sugardaddies whose eyes see
sticks of kissable honey where we see ankles, knees.
She tells me: 'To him my tiny teats are gobstoppers,
(his real name's Herbert)
my irises are bullseyes, my bodily dirt his sweetest sherbet'.

1972

Mornings, the monks loom over us
in black cassocks, scorch our palms
with leathers crafted by proud saddlers,

rip hair from our scalps like harvest.
Later we wound one another by the dozen
with pointed sticks and shaved flint, thrown

for anger and sport. Once, rough rope
burnt my wrists as my eyes averted,
the better not to see your kidneys

and liver kicked over and over,
the Barracka boys laughing, joking
they're polishing their boots on your sides.

Evenings, from the corner of the living-room,
the little black box makes dulcet announcements:
the latest Belfast bomb-blasts, riots

and rubber bullets, the balletic movements
of fire-spitting gunships over Southeast Asia.
You know, things men do.

THE MONUMENT

for Dennis O'Driscoll

Even as a child I was concerned for him:
this least triumphant of soldiers;
butt up, muzzle in the ground, ready to furrow,
helmeted head, tilted in melancholy.

On dreary days rain fell erosively on his
limestone profile, his puttees which never wetted,
his grey tunic with petrified buttons.
Was he meant to be dead or merely

sorry to have survived alone? My father
dismissed his Irishness with an uncharacteristic
whiplash of Nationalism. Was he English?
No! What was he? Lacking a spike, I knew

he couldn't be one of those Germans who
achtunged weekly across the panels of *Victor*.
Every November a wreath bloodied with poppies
lay sodden before him. On St. Patrick's Day

and Easter Sunday celebrant crowds turned
their backs to him, he who stands so faithfully
over a flaking rollcall of fusiliers' names,
McCarthy, Murphy, Prendergast, O'Sullivan:

a list as long as the road to Thurles.

Bookworm

After a lifetime of reading and book-handling
only once has a bookworm wriggled
into view, tiny and soft and scarce,
looking like an apple-riddling cousin,
but so different, so alone; the solitary
eater of words, colons, blank spaces.
His avenues of consumption led
in all different directions,
through cheap eighty gram bookwove
confined by perfect binding.

Seconds passed and with it the urge to kill,
to squash, to press the green slushy innards
out of its clothy envelope, as out of so
many caterpillars during schoolboy pogroms.
Oh, the oh too familiar blemishes, gut stains
on fingers which brought no remorse
only inexplicable satisfaction.

I went to the remainder dealer
bought twelve copies of the same
outmoded Soviet political commentary,
one hundred and twenty gram silk,
stitched bound, gold hand-tooled
titling on green cloth-bound spines,
put them all with the worm
and the half-eaten Condoleeza Rice memoir
into a draught-proof, presentation glass case.

A TIGRESS IS ...

Wood, Yang

A tigress is a girl who breakfasts
in your bed without eating you.

A tigress is a girl whose first nakedness
is the perfection of her shoulders quaking your heart.

A tigress is a girl with claws
as sharp as gentleness touching you.

A tigress is a girl with kisses
like Chinese tortures, scorching you.

A tigress is a girl with hair as russet
as the walnut scent which lulls you.

A tigress is a girl with eyes
as dark as dreamless sleep enshrouding you.

A tigress is a girl who licks up
all your purring like milk, before leaving you.

A tigress is a girl whose image
echoes in your head like a roar affrighting you.

A tigress is a girl who is camouflaged
in the jungle of her own emotions, eluding you.

ADVANCES

My poor skin affected, perplexed,
waking these mornings, you alongside, aglow,
little detonations in my limbs,
mild echoes of last night's thunder,
your caress, the measured primer.

Later you leave, your lips on my lips
but your thoughts absconding in advance
to him who cannot love you – oblivious,
like a film star luminous in a different life,
or one dead long ago.

I try decoding the debris of your departure:
Flowerpower vinyls strewn and sleeveless,
Rizla butts shedding their guts like old man's dandruff,
the spent *Avanti* lying flaccid as an afterbirth on the
wooden floor.

Forebearance

That morning I was hasty getting away.
You were naked, huddled to one side,
Your body gingerly cuddling itself.
My negligent arms were coming with me,
Out into the dry Rhodian air,
Scented with cistus, shadowed by the Acropolis.

The Church of The Panaghia was my mission;
Candles to light, indulgences to buy;
Desperation before an alien altar,
All gilt and silver and crystal,
While the Byzantine bells tolled
Through the white, corkscrew streets,
Winding their way into your sleeping mind.

Inside the church, frescoed sinners fried overhead;
Innocents were coasted on cottony clouds
To less engulfing climes. Precious metals
Framed the Virgin and her Son. I was lulled
By the perfume of beeswax burning:
And the priest began to pray,
Intoning oracles in a Greek
Even the natives failed to understand.

All through the mass
My mind was like a cobra weaving
To the rhythm of his chants
And after the wine and bread
Had been consumed I ambled home to you,
Blessed biscuits and buns to share with you,
The Grecian heat causing my every pore
To express itself, saltily, flowingly.

Brief Thoughts

On the Grand Parade
An elm's trunk bends itself.
I've watched it slowly bend for years.
Its curve is of its own design.
No shade compels
No harness constricts
The sparrows alight
no more no less
compared with straighter trees
to the left, to the right.
I think it bends to say hello
I think it bends for me;
to distract my thoughts
from other things,
outside the library.
Such as:
the rain now trickling down my nose;
the mascara you wore last night,
making threads of black,
swirling down the sink.

Measured

The way your neck inclines
as it awaits my hand's
measured touch; our skins'
unchoreographed rite which binds
tongues, eyes, waists, knees;
but it is your hands'
wilder roaming (no less
than lovers' heady bends

in deep ease) which I mean
to endure with the most
patience of a grateful man
who expects the least.

Such Things Do Happen

The flickering windows of the onrushing train,
each like a rapidly-flicked TV channel
we cannot choose to linger over.
The youngfella with streaked blue hair;

the crooning biddy with scarlet chemise
and outsized, Dalmatian hair-bow:
operas, narratives we shall never know.
Until another juncture, in a different train,

motionless in a station, dozily a carriage
pulls alongside and a solitary woman
of definitive beauty plaintively turns
her sliced almond eyes to yours.

At once astonished, each of you knows
how life should not continue like this,
alone, just as the trains start grumbling again,
in separate directions, hurriedly, without touching.

Ash Wednesday

Black lipstick ...
as if the priest's fingers had slipped.

Walking with Eliisa

Hazardous ice erupting
from the ground,
brittle stalactites
aiming themselves
from the eaves.
Along Koidula Street,
our boots crunch
the snow with a metallic ring
this wintry Ides of March.
Crows' nests lie exposed
in skeletal trees: tufts
of strange growths.
Too cold for birds to fly now
but your sweet, narrow
vowels make your voice
sound like larksong as you speak.
Reaching the tram stop
you hang by, I walk further on
leaving my blushing behind;
feeling, as if for the first time,
the cold assaulting my face.

BARE THOUGHTS IN MARIA'S BED

Like siblings we lie; you snoring,
I with eyes open to the sky.
More than twenty years have lapsed
since we were lovers, dozing,
half a lifetime of others-to-clasp awaiting us.
Their rapturous mewings lie scattered now
like seed in the wind,
as they themselves, as they themselves.
Nowadays we have only snores
in place of sighs for each other
but still we smile and rest our heads
in others' places;
their touch, their look, their scent
like phantom limbs still aching.

RILKE'S TRAVELS c. 1897

1: Venice

Exotic cries. And we select
a gondola, slender and black:
a delicate gliding, past the stakes
of a marble metropolis.

Tacit and still, the boats relate only
to one another. The oars cautiously sweep;
from out of Stygian canals and churches
an alien night beckons.

The black stakes grow imperceptable,
the breeze wafts away a faint *Ave* -
suddenly: I am a dead emperor
and they guide me to my tomb.

2: Arco

The towering pinnicles of snow, jagged and pointed,
flare up like a crowned wall
into which the laughing Nero
of morning casts his flare.

And as the flames blend to azure
the fated stars of evening fade away.
the valley erupts into a beautiful terror
and plunges upwards out of dream and dew.

3: I Mulini

You weary, decaying mill
your mossed wheel rests peacefully,
from out of the olives' coolness,
evening watches over you.

The brook makes noises
like the songs of lost persons,
deeper over your ears
you draw your resisting roof.

4: Konstanz

The day is so fey, weariness
flows from golden communion cups,
wine soaks into the mountain snow.

High-up over the water's edge,
coy as a roe, a star is timorous,
while ornamental shivering wavelets
lattice the sea.

5: Bodensee

The villages are like posies of flowers.
In spires of peculiar origin
the bells peal like pain.
Shoreline castles mark time
and gaze through black embrasures,
weary of the midday sea.

Swelling waves frisk and frolic
and golden steamers gently
careen in the open current
and beyond the horizon
the multitudinous summits
rise and rise to the surface.

Apollanaire's Annie

On the coastline of Texas
between Mobile and Galveston
there nestles an enormous garden
riddled with roses. And in its centre
a mansion, itself a rose.

A woman promenades there
among these roses, totally alone.
And when I pass by,
on the lime-boundried dirt-road,
we regard each other.

As a complying Mennonite
her bushes are budless, her blouse button-free.
On my own frayed-sleeved coat, two little polythene discs,
have loosened their threads and rolled away,
making her and me, almost of the same mind.

In the Sculpture Room of the Crawford Art Gallery

I never had the chalky whiteness
of Teucer, the archer, whose buttocks
arched with the rigidity of a bow.
My biceps never bulged when casting a spear,

or grappling with a many-coiled serpent.
Now if I struck a pose of bow-plucking,
my navel would obscure my fig-leaf
from the sun's bright, glorious balm.

In a corner, a languid, stricken Cupid
is comforted by a pretty Psyche,
opiately-oblivious to the wounds
of her snapped-off, mislaid wings.

The drunken faun twists his spine
the better to gaze at the rage
of a Roman battle-frieze overhead,
while boy-Mercury pauses to stare

at his held-high arm, as if thereon
an invisible butterfly still hovered,
as if Vesuvius froze him in this moment.
Not everyone's tragedy is so beautiful:

does handless William Pitt know
he's exiled to unsympathetic Cork?
William Crawford's slothful girth
is gifted camouflage by Hogan's

draping of a marble cloak
in folds, like still-malleable icing,
inedible for Cork's unartistic poor.
Patronage always did prefer subterfuge.

In a room full of coy naked boys
and sporty, shameless men, Heffernan
and I are the only admirers of women.
His Susannah sits at the bath

as shy as she is slim. After two centuries
of waiting for a towel there are no drips on her.
Amid the envious observation of perfect bodies
I suddenly remember the simple heroism

on that hot Rhodian strand, of the one-breasted woman,
her chest imbalanced by a cruciform scar,
and realise, beauty comes in other forms too:
like the fitful stirrings of Davoren in my arms

blue-eyed and blond, his butterfly lashes
kissing my astonished cheek.

Indirect from Decleor

Mornings, my hair stands shocked
thin peaks of grey flames poised
to scorch to ash any naive soul
who might glimpse them.

The beauty nymphs slumber still
in the wall-cracks around me
heads resting on bedbugs for pillows
the same damned bedbugs

I've been unable to poison
since the mail-ordered nymphs
moved-in, shacked up.
Impatient, envious, I thump the walls

why should I be insomnia's solitary victim
engine to a thousand night-time anxieties.
I sit here dark and brooding,
a separate weather system in the rumpled

mountain range of my bedclothes
before thumping the walls again
buckling the cheap veneer cladding
forcing the nymphs out of their holes.

They stream like screeching miniature bats.
My skin's flaky patches are rapidly spat upon
then polished by a thousand invisible wings.
A million bombard my head with perfumed guano

styling the entire luminous morass
into the latest post-Vidal Sassoon
pre-whatever formation.
The red whips streaking from irises

across the whites of my eyeballs
are massaged into temporary invisibility.
And eventually I stand before the mirror
without danger of it cracking,

marvelling at the memory of distant days
when I looked like this, better, 24 hours a day
sleep or no sleep, no veneer,
no bedbugs, no nymphs, no anxieties.

Replacing Old Taps

My poet's wordstore cuts no conduits
at the plumbers' emporium:
speaking of 'the *khiasmos* of pipes
laid by an amateur, flaking with excrescence,

rivulating through my domicile',
I know, will win me no eager service.
So I vice my tongue and try to remember
how that oversized wedding-ring of brass

is called an 'olive', to stanch
the dripping drupes squeezing onto
my floors: a transparent, viscous
harvest I could live without.

Stacks and shelves of basins, siphons,
retaining nuts, augers, cisterns,
taps, compression joints, await
the jaded eyes of rough-handed regulars.

For me they are thingamajigs and whatsits.
The soft-eyed apprentice maintains
his patience with a barely discernible sigh
as yet another inarticulate do-it-yourself

time-waster stiffly approaches him.
I communicate my needs with hand gestures
and a technical pidgin, all the while oblivious
to the marvellous metaphoric possibilities

of stopcocks and diaphragm valves,
gully grills and plungers.

The Poet Contemplates Book Cover Portraits

Twenty-two years old

I know already I've written the poems
that fat-faced fucker will take credit for,
the anthologised gems on love and death.
When they're published in the *Selected*
I want my young, lean visage to stare out
at the reader perusing the back cover.
Let them know *I* wrote them and not
the balding, greying git who gets
the credit and the royalty cheque
as modest as his girth is wide.

Forty-two years old

I hate those poets who choose
photos ten years old or more
to adorn the covers of their latest
slim outputs, especially those who
write on love and sex, advertising
themselves to potential new conquests
as fresh-faced and full-coloured.
I think for my next book
I'll feature the best of Fyffes,
captioned: 'Portrait of the Poet as a Banana'.
A little jaundiced-looking, perhaps,
but still good enough to eat.

Purchased Wisdom

for Håken Sandell

sinking, as if stood on fish, my feeling.
Rilke, *The Book of Images*

Your body I strewed in cleft steaks,
your rended head lay calmed before me.
A spray of scales sprinkled the counter's top
their weight and judgement eyeing me sorely.

No ritual of manly hunting brought you
to my kitchen door, no olive quill
exquisitely tied, no errif nondescript
hooked you skilfully by lip or gill.

Trapped in the farm, the sea's taste,
dropped by wind, provoked a yearning
greater than the urge to spurt roe:
a want for frondy crevices, spurning

the bare, barless cage of the sterile pool.
Passing clouds were dreams of wild shoals
of succulent offerings moister than
the crisp feed the farmer shovels.

Rain fell like a discontinuous river
you couldn't swim. The sun's glare
was the Salmon God's blessing;
a metaphysical balm to ease the sear

of loneliness: the Atlantic leaper
who was your destiny found another.
The courtly combat with gallant angler
you never knew, just the smother

of air the farmer soused you in.
All I hope is my small son's cheeks imbibe
the healthy hues of fish I poorly bought;
your wisdom shield him from sly diatribe.

Laurence Corcoran 1910–1995

My grandfather never spoke with oysters in his mouth
and always rhymed that tee-haytch word with gout,
a sickness which never afflicted anyone he knew.
When he spoke of barley, the broad *ahhhs*

and burred *rrrrs* of Shakespeare were perfectly preserved
behind teeth which never touched a malt.
The monotonous rhythms of factory noise
bludgeoned his ears till he was deaf.

The world changed its accent around him.
His pedigreed, plebeian assonance sing-songed
all the days that all about him adjusted their tongues
like aerials to the Montrose English of flickering grey screens.

He was as honest as his speech
and rich in all the things which honesty brings:
children bustled around him
like brokers at an exchange.

At his graveside I let fall all airs,
prayed and wailed like a Coal Quay shawlie.

MARGARET CORCORAN (NÉE KIRWIN)

Your voice was good enough
to make cabbages flourish.
It drifted like a nourishing mist
over the market-garden field behind.

One neighbour stopped herself
fingering piano to listen to you.
Others drained the sound and light
from their wireless sets.

Your voice had no coach
other than the rhythms of your daily chores;
the wringing of clothes soaked by hand;
the conveyer-belt of nappies; cramming of mouths.

Every day your husband thanked his god;
counted his blessings: you and his nine babies,
their hair sprouting as luxuriant
as the cabbage leaves they might

have been stashed and found behind.
Your voice was good enough for marble halls,
for slow boats to China,
for moving through the fair.

Your voice was the balm of all our childhoods.
I*s there anything you would have done differently?*
I would have taken singing lessons, you said,
striking a different note.

Forebear

Everything that glittered in this world
turned to cinders when he touched it.
His young wife's smile
disappeared from her face until she was old.
The Grattan Hill house bequeathed by his grandfather
turned inside out storm after storm.
Bottles of whiskey lost the gold of their gleam
swallow by swallow when left near his hands.

A scoundrel cousin
had stolen away with the family baronetcy.
Steadily and completely his sobriety vanished
until one morning he awoke
beside the Queenstown railway line
to discover half his beard was missing,
shorn off by the screeching wheels
which had failed to waken him.

NIGHTFEED

for Romy

I am the funnel of uncountable mutations
You are my destination, my culmination
aeons of genes replicated to reach you

If I were deaf to your wails
my nose could sniff you out
by your subtle, Gubeen aroma.

Feeding, your eyelids flicker open
like a moth's unfolding wings
and the moon is a jewel

reflected in your pupils.
The plastic sceptre of diminishing white
is clasped between my finger and thumb

as the vice of your toothless gums
chews relentlessly.

Somewhere in the city,
with bricks of my nana's heart,
my baby aunts' coughs lie stifled by clay.

Each morning I lay awake,
my ears pricked
for the gift of your grunts.

Wereteen

Sometimes a saw turns to song,
sometimes a song turns to sawing.
My son's voice breaks,
his pretty child pitch droned out
by a stranger's bass protest.
Only now can I accept my father's dismay
when he saw his soft-eyed boy
morph into a creature ranker than a dog,
breaking out with bristles all over.
He would skulk past my bedroom
as past a death to be ignored,
pine after the pet who had sat on his lap,
who had marked him with kisses.
On nights the moon shone
he stuffed rags to the gap under my door
the better to muffle the howls,
the unseasonal scratchings of wood,
the stench of unstoppable effusions.

Confessions of a Nightporter

It's odd falling in and out of sleep,
feeling the sleep curl this way and that
through your brain like a wave,
like a heavy syrup swirling slowly
through the hollow chamber of a seashell.
It happens when you need to keep your wits about you
like when a bird sleeps with one eye closed
and one eye opened. Except when you're human
you can't do it that way. Both eyes need to be shut
and the sleep undulates with every sound
and every silence.

Party for Innocents, May 1971

to Paul, Carol, Michael, Marcus and I.M. Aidan

St. Maries of the Isle School,
My memories as lazy as dreams
I gather up scenes as from a cutting room floor.
Our legs were slender and delicate like saplings.
Blousy white first communicants giggled feverishly
Or flitted about, fluffy and fleeting as dandelion seed.
Sisters of Mercy, black as aged crows,
Smiled wistfully on, soulwithered by nostalgia.
Tartrazine-hued drinks are what I like to recall
And crusty crumbs of blue icing
Which tickled their way up our shirtsleeves.

When we left the hall a busload of waiting Americans.
Fat and bespectacled, delivered a broadside of *Kodak* and *Canon* fire.
We posed diffidently, an incongruous, provincial *Our Gang.*
With each shuttersnap our lines were etched invisibly
On black negative by the sun; to be processed
Into otherworldly monochrome or richman's Technicolor.
As I skipped my way home my amber rosette was fanned
Like the sunlight spreading down through the cathedral spires.

Somewhere now, spread out through distant America
Lie a dozen photographs, untraceable records,
Curled and collecting dirt,
Their photographers are dead or centenarian.
Many of their subjects are bearded or pregnant.
One little innocent is long since dust:
An uneasy pillion-rider crushed into tarmac.

Soul After Death

after Håken Sandell

Only now is it clear, my body was as a warming sun,
left cold latterly by the darkness of light's abstractions.
I miss the body and blood's warmth.
I miss my ashen complexion and dawn's
stuttering cough, heart causing the arteries to surge
in enormous flood beneath my shades of autumn,
tattoos soft as silken cloth. In the decrepit bones,
in spite of everything, vestigial youth still rejoiced.
My shoulders contained all the power of wings.
A seraphic shrine encased the pig-like skin.
On the wrist, the miniature, model world of the watch
contained hours of exhilarating depth.
The minutes pulsated more than eternal stars.
I miss the brain's perceived stability, a jewel
of clarity, miss the breathing caged in my ribs,
the cock's hardness, the muscles which flex
in strength, blood streaming to my hands,
to return, as in the limbs of the crucified
and air that is fine and aged and ephemeral
flowing into the lungs once more.
Every scar a precious memory abandoned now
with the wedding band bound fast to the finger
and the body itself, so soon obliterated.

LAST DAY

When the trumpet called
I made for the ancestral graveyard,
waited ten minutes before resurrection
before slitting my throat;
did it just as I've always pictured it,
one swift slice of the jugular
with an even-weighted black-handled blade.
As the skin parted on my neck
my heart jumped to my throat
where for a few too-long seconds
it pumped harder the remaining blood
which hadn't yet drained.
Poor heart felt like bursting with its own pain.
Blackness descended on my brain as capillaries dried.
I was dazed and drowsy when minutes later
the corpuscles leapt back into my throat
like miniature scarlet salmon.
Stumbling naked women, dusted with earth
arose around me and sang aloud
plaintive songs of return, songs of imploring
for their missing tresses of youth.
A few feet away, a murdered American, never identified,
wondered about the whereabouts of his absent prepuce.
'How is this thing supposed to work?' he asked,
'Does it come to me, or must I go back to Vermont
to collect it?'
I shrugged my shoulders in response,
… or was I just in spasm?

THE GARDEN

1: The Manufacture of Replicas

The boy surveys the dream-potential
of the plentiful blue bell.
Each seed-loaded jewel:
an unopened factory
of blue perfume,
enough to blanket an entire suburb,
with beacons for bees and botonists,
and other connoisseurs of scent.
The boy sprawls in a carpet of coltsfoot,
his eyes shimmering
at the diamond-studded sky above.
His senses reaching-out to the fragrance
of a girl he has never met,
quietly asleep in a distant house,
her smooth, folded knees
guarding the unripe nectar
he'll someday reap.

2: Confessions of a Ten-year-old Sadist

No snakes exist:
so the boy slithers;
exploiting a breach
in the garden of night,
His path's illuminated by candlelight.
Beetles fall prey
to his gathering-box,
aphids are extinguished
with ether.
The Stygian mirrors
of the boy's eyes
reflect the flowers of fire,
the seed heads of dandelions
exploding into flame
like a sequence of planets;
their globes of blue blaze
ignited by the candle's
flickering touch.
As a dozen dandelion souls
flee spritely to limbo,
the boy's soul
quivers like a budgerigar
in a cold cage.

3: War Colours

The boy's made privy to war's atrocities.
His stomach lies shivering on insidious grass,
wet, killer, kidney-stifling grass.

A horde of snails oozes over a bed of blossoms:
sliming precious Persian Jewels,
Livingston Daisies, Love-in-a-mist.
They chomp and chew through a village of lilies.

At cool, anaemic sunrise
a floral Mai-Lai lies ragged in their slow-motion wake.
Bolts of bridal cloth glisten silvery over the wounded stems.

4: The Revenge of the Lilies

The boy plots with grieving lilies:
What are the fears which snails share?
Being landlord to a wasp in one's shell.
Being mistaken for a bumpkin periwinkle.
Being spotted with a polka-dot foot.
Being informed one is no longer hermaphrodite.
Being fed for life on a diet of thistles.
Being naked as a slug in the Sahara desert.
Being tested for Dr. Marten's new, stamp-smart,
nightvision boot.
Being buried in salt.
Being antlerless after a fight with a black scissors.
Being serenaded by a crow singing 'Shelltyhorn,
Shelltyhorn'
Being acquainted with the verb *manger*.

5: Song and Aerial Dance

The boy's minute:
he rides on a magpie's wing.
They go in hunt
of every glittering thing.
They snatch a button
from a Woolworth girl's coat;
then a blue-bottle's back;
then a *Tanora* can's discarded ring,
before they themselves are ensnared
on the vervals of music;
They dive to its source:
the ice-cream man's van,
swerving at the last instant into the sky,
repelled by the coldness of memory.

As compensense the magpie relates
a certain blackbird song:

'How small a word is tree
how much bigger is rustle
which the tiniest leaf sings'.

6: A Bedtime Story

In dream
the clouds are heedless of the trees:
they seep down quietly
through the budding twigs
and scoop me up, swathing me
in their wooly wetness.
The brusque winds shepherd us
to where they want us to flow,
blowing us
over moonglistening oceans
and cities which glint
with a million eyes of cats.

7: Prophecy

In slumber, the boy succumbs to a toxic dream:
Starlings lie impaled on whitethorn
their reddening breasts mistaken for haws
by hungry jackdaws.

His window admits a noose of bindweed
to rhythmicly envelop his throat,
its porcelain blossoms are pharos seeping with poison.

Lace curtains throw shadow nets to capture his sight
as he dreams he awakens.

And then he does
and all is quiet
except his heart.

8: The Lure of Night

The boy knows his last summer has come
and listens intently
to the sadnesses of automobiles;
their lonely wails; their frustrated screeches.
He sits alone in his parents' garden
beneath the mooncast shade
of the youngest sycamore.
The tree has fruited for the first time,
not because the boy is dying,
but because it is simply time.
The older trees applaud.
They have angels between their leaves,
playing with their seed.
A horseshoe is dipping, rising,
confused in its eddy of being.
The boy dreams he is king
of this backyard sliver of greenland.
He dreams he wears a jade crown;
a wreath of greenfly, that the ants and bees
respect his sovereignty, that this summer night
continues for an eternity.

9: In the End

In the end his eyes
would be the dandelion's
bright corona,

his ear the foxglove's
tubular petal.

His fingernails
would be subsumed in scutch,

his hair
in the tendrils of clematis.

His heart would be
the apple-worm's browned-off feast,

his brain the scrunched
bulb of the crocus.

His soul the mist
conferring dew on all.

About the Author

Patrick Cotter was born in Cork in 1963 where he continues to live and work as director of the Munster Literature Centre. He has published poems in numerous periodicals, anthologies and chapbooks including *A Misogynist's Blue Nightmare* (Dublin, Raven Arts Press, 1990) and *The True Story of Aoife and Lir's Children* (Cork, Three Spires Press, 2002). His translations of various German poets have been published in journals and his translations of the Estonian Surrealist poet Andres Ehin were collected in *Moosebeetle Swallow* (Cork, Southword Editions, 2005). Cotter's own poems have been translated and published in Italy, Spain and Sweden. *Återuppståndelser* (Resurrections), a small selection of Cotter's poems translated into various Scandinavian languages, was published in Gothenburg in 2007. His work has been shortlisted for both the Hennessy Award and the Patrick Kavanagh Award.

Perplexed Skin is his début collection.